The Second Week
of the Soap

Fiona Ritchie Walker

Red Squirrel Press

First published in the UK in 2013 by
Red Squirrel Press
Briery Hill Cottage
Stannington
Morpeth
Northumberland
NE61 6ES
United Kingdom
www.redsquirrelpress.com

Red Squirrel Press is distributed by Central Books and
represented by Inpress Ltd.
www.inpressbooks.co.uk

Cover photograph by Anne Witton
www.annewitton.org.uk

A CIP record for this book is available
from The British Library.

ISBN 9781906700683

Printed by Martins the Printers.
Seaview Works
Spittal
Berwick-upon-Tweed
TD15 1RS
United Kingdom

Acknowledgements

Thanks are due to the editors of the following publications where some of these poems first appeared:

Anthologies
Bite Me, Robot Dog (Dog Horn Publishing); *Blood Lines* (Blinking Eye); *New Writing 15* (British Council/Granta); *New Writing Scotland 23, 24, 25, 28, 29 & 30* (ASLS); *Rowing Home* (Cruse); *Ten Years On* (New Writing North).

Magazines
The Battered Suitcase; BBC Gardeners' World; Citizen 32; Drey; The London Magazine, Mslexia, The Red Wheelbarrow.

Websites
Basil Bunting Award and Second Light
Poetry Advent Calendar

The Glass River was commissioned by Threshold Theatre to celebrate the life of Githa Sowerby as part of the festival marking the premiere of her play, *Rutherford & Son,* on its native Tyneside.

Several poems have won prizes in competitions including Mslexia, Inpress Books, Millwheel Writers, Alan Sillitoe Poetry Competition, and the Barnet Open Poetry Competition. *Mrs Thorpe's Arithmetic* won the BBC Gardeners' World Magazine Poetry Competition in 2012 and was broadcast on Radio 4's *Poetry Please.*

Thanks to Jamie Hince and Alison Mosshart of the Kills, whose interview in Harper's Bazaar inspired the poem, *Marion County.*

Thanks to Sheila Wakefield, Jeanne Macdonald, Kathleen Kenny, Peter Collins, Carte Blanche writing group and my family for encouragement and support.

For David

Contents

Dhaka at Midnight

No street lights.
High above, electric cables
skein across the sky.

A boy on a ladder
unhooks one,
throws it down.

When you stop
the crowd watch you
watching them.

You do not see
the black snake, its naked wires
unspinning by your sandals.

When sparks snap in the puddle
you think only of fireworks and bonfires,
imagine the gasp is for someone else,

not this pale stranger
walking through the charged water.

Masks

When you say *masks*
I'm thinking carnival,
smells from the hot food stalls

and last night's quickening drums,
those women dancing
in the narrow streets.

By the sacred river
it's the flower garlands that catch my eye,
not the scar of boots on the shore.

I want to stop
when the chai stall overturns
and metal cups clatter in the steam.

Those barked warnings
from the megaphone
are words that I don't know.

I'm still thinking photographs
and something new to see
when you say *run*.

Through the Car Window

A boy steers his leashed monkey
up and down the dhaba tables.

A man drinking chai glances up,
the boy nods his head.

The monkey somersaults
to the top of the boy's stick.

The boy presses his fingers together
as in prayer.

The monkey presses its fingers together
as in prayer.

The man rises,
throws rupees on the table.

The monkey picks up the coins,
hands them to the boy.

Last I see they are at the counter,
the lady handing over two cigarettes.

Jackfruit

On the first day of the honey month he buys me jackfruit,
places it on the ledge of our bedroom window.

The same day, while he is working, she phones our home,
says his name, sweet like his mother's tea.

I hear her breath draw back sharp
through her reddened lips as my own voice replies.

On the third day of the honey month I wait for him
to tell me of the letter but his voice stays silent.

The jackfruit sits like a green spiked pig, watching
his empty side of the bed. I count minutes towards daylight.

In our room the smell begins to change. From the ledge rises
the warm decay that signals ripe fruit within.

On the tenth day of the honey month he tells me
I am lazy and ungrateful. I have wasted his generous gift.

Its soft, milky moons, fragrant like the nights he promised,
are now rotting round their slimy stones.

In the Covered Market

We were looking for shelter
from the monsoon rains, shivered
between stalls of cleavered meat,
ducks stripped of feathers.

You said snake, mistaking zigzag scales.
Three fish lay in a blue bowl,
soft-shelled crabs tumbled
like clockwork toys.

We bought dragonfruit and soursop
which we would leave in our hotel room,
untasted, untouched
for lack of a knife.

You laughed when I took home
the gaudy paper money
and origami shoes,
unaware they were offerings.

When you and the Perfume River
were just memories,
I carried all that remained

beyond the flowerbeds, struck the match.

Pablo's Instructions for Travel

The man is green here as in your home,
not like Buenos Aires where he walks in white.
And when it is your turn it is also for the traffic
but even though they are coming, don't stop.
Walk as if you mean it. Don't take for granted
the direction. Here in Santiago it changes in the day.
Maybe you can take the subway, buy a *boleto*,
it will stay in the machine, not like London.

Look here, you see the Andes are missing.
So much smog. Our yellow buses,
exhausting line after line. Much crowded,
watch your bags. And wear your dark glasses
to hide your blue eyes.
All our bus system changes tomorrow, so much
confusion. Yes, you could travel on one then.
Like you, no-one will know what they are doing.

Sunday, the City of Rivers

Don't miss the sea wolves, the hotel clerk said.
They lay along the bank like rolled-up carpets.
Above them, men filleted and chopped,
throwing scraps from their stalls without looking.

One pelican caught a fish head in flight,
but most trimmings fell to the sea wolves
who swayed to the movement of knives
then swam upstream to flounder out,
lie in the sun to dry.

A man staggered,
blew a whistle close to their faces
and my hand, with its camera, rose.

I could not translate what the passer-by said
but I knew his meaning. One day
this drunk would lose his hand, perhaps an arm.

A woman nudged me,
take a photo anyway,
but my fingers refused to move.

Walking back through the market
I bought one old peso,
shaped and stamped with Mapuche seasons,
threaded on a chain.

Caught in sunlight,
the silver glints like scales.

(Sea wolves – South American sea lions)

Hotel Gran Sucre

In a moment
you will walk across the pitted floor
and the silence.
The stooped man will appear
with a plate of melon
and you will ask in your halting Spanish
for a *cortado*,
though the coffee he brings
will be instant and black.

For now
you are trying to decide
which table in this emptiness
will be yours,
where is the best vantage point
to see the carved staircase at its best
to imagine the brides
and the bands
and the dancing.

The Palm Trees of Curico

You have decided, during the ten-hour bus ride
without air conditioning, that you must photograph
the palm trees of Curico.
The guide book says, apart from tasting wine,
that this is the thing to do.

So because your bag is light
and your ticket cheap, transferable,
when the conductor says *Curico*,
you peel yourself from the plastic seat
and stand behind the woman with the striped shopping bag,
peer inside it at something feathered and still.

You have decided the plaza with the palm trees
lies to the left, maybe because of the angle
of the sun, or perhaps you are drawn
by the man snipping greenery into a swan.

You sit on a bench, recognise
the lack of palms in the dusty square,
ignore the dog with the swollen tongue.

There is a key by your feet.
Hotel Ivanetta, Room 201.
Not listed in the guidebook but there,
to the right of the park, is the sign.
To go to reception, explain your discovery,
that's what you intend. But the dog
bounds up the stairs and you follow,
turning right to find
a door with the number that's in your hand.

Someone has left a postcard on the bed.
The Plaza at Curico. Its magnificent palms.
You are holding this when the maid uses
her master key, asks in her own language
how long you are staying.

All your phrases have gone, except
lightly grilled, the bill please, and *tomorrow,*
so you point to the postcard and she shakes her head,
picks up a leaflet showing this is not Curico.
The guide book says this town is famous
for its topiary, except in years of drought.

You should have photographed the green swan.
You should not have said to the maid
the bill please, tomorrow.

You should have stopped the dog
from chewing the bedspread.
But there is wine
and tomorrow, maybe Curico.

For Those Who Make the Arpilleras

In the unseasonal rain
I dream of you women,
your invisible hands
steering this long thin ship*,
the glide of your scissors and needles,
this gentle re-telling of history
with no movement of your faces,
the way you say
we at the soup kitchen could not speak out.
We turned skirts and blouses into pictures
that told of our frustrations.
These became our voices.

In this unseasonal rain
I dream of you, Margarita,
who sewed to put your children
through higher education
and Adriana, making lunch for your sick neighbour.
I hear your strong voices
drumming on Santiago's rooftops,
because of this
we have learned a different reality.

*Long thin ship - Pablo Neruda's description of Chile

The Lima House

We went upstairs only
to show me the neighbourhood
beneath the donkey-belly sky,
stood together at the window
with its yellowed tape, trapped tinsel.

Books had been thrown in the corner
of the abandoned room.
How many languages?

A first aid kit, door open,
bandages in a neat row.
Over the fireplace a clean circle.
Pinned to its left, a calendar,
all the months gone.

Two lamps, a chandelier
and on the landing,
a stained glass boat
frozen in a dusty sea.

Down the servants' stairs,
a kettle sat on the rusted stove,
heavy with old water.

Leaving

A thundering like rain
but nothing wet.

Cattle kissed, untied.
We slap them towards freedom.

I carry a pot of salt,
our silver spoon.

The baby bounces in my mother's shawl,
rags over his eyes.

Mr de Souza bound six hives to his oxcart before dawn.
Now bees dance round our faces.

Crossing the river, he stumbles.
His ankle twists like a weeping fig.

I bite the hem of my petticoat,
use a strip to stem his bleeding.

The pot floats downstream,
salt dissolves.

The baby chews on the spoon,
throws it to the ground.

Mr de Souza is heavy against my shoulder.
Between his cries, I hear scorched stones crack.

Aftershock

What has happened to the bar in Cauquenes
where we ate salted pork
from a gnarled wood platter
and tasted wine
made with grapes you had grown.

And what has happened to the shuttered room
where cool linen covered the table
and we speared our conversation
with green olives.

The sweetness of papayas
as we watched fishing boats depart.

Somewhere I have that photograph
of the seaweed stalls.
Behind them, crested waves
and the deep blue you said
was the colour you longed to wear
around your head and shoulders.

Journey

They say it was a boat no bigger than a balcony,
that she set off under a spilt milk sky,
sugar rain spattering,
nothing too wet to sit on.

That day the land was a sandwich
barnacled by the concrete sea,
in the marram, the forgotten wingspan
of a gull, the black dog.

They say she knew nothing of fog, winds, tide,
that there's grey on the rocks, hair,
a full head of it, and there, where the wind catches,
her tiny patch of dry.

Driving to Skukuza

They came across buffalo, horns locked,
in the middle of the road.

Unsure how the beasts would react to the vehicle,
or the agreed excess in the car hire agreement,
they sat with their cameras switched on
though the morning sun
blinded the automatic exposure.

They listened to the battle,
horn on horn,
while she flicked through the book
for guidance but found only
their proper name: syncerus caffer.

Between each clash the buffalo rubbed
their thick-skinned faces together,
the one on the right nuzzling into what she would call
the other's nape and closing its eyes.

And she felt a stirring in her own throat,
a rising pain, solid as bone, or the twist
of a battle-scarred horn, as she realised
she did not know much about buffalo,

for instance, whether these two, now so symmetrical
against the sun, were male or
one male and a mate, sparring
over something small, maybe as small as
apertures or film speed
but then finding in the fight
something tender, familiar,

so that despite the angle of the sun and all she knew
about the rules of light and composition,
she pressed the button, making the shutter blink
before he fired up the ignition
to move them on.

Northern Territory

We were at the lake's edge, nothing for fifty miles.
September and the first freeze glinting between wet stones,
a death crackle in the still green leaves.
Sudden sun, we launched the canoe, headed west.

September and the first freeze glinting between wet stones.
You said the spirit took our June memory, turned it into today,
sudden sun. We launched the canoe, headed west,
boomeranging back to the first time we met.

You said the spirit took our June memory, turned it into today.
Your mouth teaching me those blunt Chipewyan vowels,
boomeranging back to the first time we met.
I try not to count the days.

Your mouth teaching me those blunt Chipewyan vowels,
us picking cranberries, no sugar to make jam.
I try not to count the days,
watch the wooden pier ice over.

Us picking cranberries, no sugar to make jam,
a death crackle in the still green leaves.
Watch the wooden pier ice over.
We were at the lake's edge, nothing for fifty miles.

Glacier

She listens carefully to the instructions.
Use the ice axe, keep the rope taut,
never turn feet sideways.

She watches the rope stretch, hears dark slush
crunch beneath careful strides, a relentless rhythm,
the pull of those before and behind.

She wants to stop, to look at the ice,
the patches of pure glass,
that sea of frozen ripples.

Swirls of blue spiral down. She stretches to see
the bottom. The sun is widening the water lozenges,
she must watch where she is stepping.

Above, where blue meets blue,
a distant avalanche,
the top so unstable no-one can climb there.

Time to head down but first
one last upward look,
the rope pulling, crack deepening,

her wet stumble, ice
freezing skin,
a rush so loud

she cannot hear the others calling
through all those frozen colours.
Her very own kaleidoscope.

The Secret Life of Feet

I treat them well, pedicures and creams,
a touch of varnish on summer days
and still they choose to leave.
Not openly, putting on those high heels
and tapping down the hall,
but stealthily while I sleep.

Sometimes I wake at midnight,
imprisoned on the bed.
I worry about speeding cars, broken glass,
feel my spirits lift each morning
when I pull back the duvet to find them
returned, dust on their thick-skinned soles.

I wish they could be trusted
but they go their own way.
Last night they persuaded my legs
to join them, found gravel
to sting my knees,
five round bruises for my thigh.

He Tells Me

Dream yourself back before birth.
Reappear as a kite
reckless with harlequin colours
and a ribbon, slippy with unravelling.

Live in another language.
Translate the past
and arrange by syllables.

Even the smallest word
has its own hue,
a place within the rainbow.

Memories lie
like seeds in cold earth
with no set time or season.

Remember how you taught yourself
to love the taste of olives.

Marion County

We were so wide eyed back then,
taking Polaroids of ourselves every morning,
remembering the unmade bed, the open window,
other weather hidden over the horizon.

Taking Polaroids of ourselves every morning
along the dirt track hugging the cliff,
other weather hidden over the horizon.
Everything now in monochrome.

Along the dirt track hugging the cliff,
squinting into the tangerine sun.
Everything now in monochrome -
we are late, we are always late.

Squinting into the tangerine sun,
remembering the unmade bed, the open window,
we are late, we are always late.
We were so wide eyed back then.

This song

is red.
Flaps like a flag.
There's a hint
of exhaust fumes
around its edges,
a base of patchouli.

These notes sing silver,
dulling to pewter,
black.

Here I'm seeing
a turned field,
now it's barley
and above it August blue.

Something's flying.
That's the beat of a wing
or it could be pale
butter falling from a churn.

This chorus,
tart as apples,
high kicks
in red stilettos
across a marble floor.

Somewhere
I've lost the title.
I'll be humming
red all day.

The Artist's Commission

It was a wild December sea,
there was no light.
Seagulls sheltered on land,
spray filled the sky.

His hands bled
and this fine jacket on his back
was an old, ripped cloak
he pulled from the hook
before running to the shore.

She was never this beautiful
and she swore worse than the men,
but her hair was black
and the lighthouse beam that dim.

You will point her out with your cigar,
dinner guests will admire her painted calm.

I will buy potatoes,
perhaps cheap wine,
pay the rent.

On Canvas

When I look at my dress I smell mint,
think toothpaste, see the big sausage
of gloopy white he squeezes onto the palette
and though I know I should be breathing
turps and dust, I picture fresh, white teeth.

When I look at his windows, rectangles
of light in the black walls and eaves,
I can't find the housey smells:
scented candles, fresh coffee,
hot starch from a ticking iron.

Even now, in this new scene, when
the air should have a note of garlic,
hibiscus and Mediterranean blue,
I'm taking in that back-of-the-hand skin
smell as he brings the brush next to what will,
in a moment, be the inside of my thigh.

I'd love to ask him what he thinks
should be my perfume, what he would sniff
if he came close to my face, nuzzled in below
the curve of my still-wet ear.

Only now, before I start to go
from liquid, to sticky, to dry
could he know the real fragrance
of my heart. By the time I'm framed
and on the wall, I'll be odourless, flat.

The Man and the Moon

"It is popularly believed that forage crops
should be sowed during the dark of the moon."
Pliny the Elder

He only worked girls.
Took each new lass
on a tour of his fields,
told her of the moon,
390 times closer than the sun,
how even the land rose and fell
at its turning.

Wax and plant.

He rang the bell outside the bothy,
wife back home asleep
as they scurried along the lane
single file, yawning
ready to bury midnight seeds
cosy down the plantlings.

Wane and prune.

Some thought it daft,
a few agreed the cut ends
bled less sap.

The moon marked out their year.
Wolf, snow, crust, corn.

They watched for Saturn,
planted perennials.
Closed the shutters
when the old moon lay
in the arms of the new.

Their own bodies fell in
with the lunar pull
as they ripped rags together
to catch the bleeding.

On dormant nights
they curled in their low bunks waiting.
For the squeak of the door.
For the round face peering in.
For his heavy breathing.

The Letting

At seven months my daughter bit me,
drew blood, kept feeding.
When she started walking and grazed her arm
she licked it clean. When it rained
she picked worms from the wet earth,
carried them in her pockets.

At seventeen she walked past the men,
scooped up the breathing
mass of bloodied feathers,
brought them home.

Now, night after night I scrub her linen,
fade the blood.

Some say she is possessed,
walking the woods and pond line
until her legs are darkened with feeding bodies,
but those whose wounds are healed,
humours balanced,
welcome her to their bedside.

I watch her with her charges. See how
she opens the box when business is slow,
strokes their shining, hungry thinness,
lets them suckle on her wrists and ankles.

The Glass River

A poetry sequence to celebrate the life and work
of Gateshead playwright Githa Sowerby

Fusing

You came into a world
of soda, sand and lime
fuelled with Northern fire.

And though the Sowerby mould
made angels of the house
to add lustre in the gloom,
pull worn boots from masters,

you poured water on these vitric ways,
embraced their state
of solid solution, knowing
not everything is compound,

pencil and paper could work as well as iron,
would shatter and shape old world ways,
frit them with newfound women's voices.

Flow

As if the current changed direction
  and poured free from its casting,
kept its rich filling, the Gateshead nuggets,
  deep within the gather.

        As if the Tyne veined south
        beneath the scarred land,
          merged into the Thames
        where you sat in the boat, writing.

As if the river gullied across the city
  that first month of the great unrest,
found a new course centre stage,
  led you to the empty Embankment,

        to walk with applause
        rippling in your head,
          acclaim in the morning editions
        you would carry home.

Flux

No cullet.
Nothing connecting.

You chose to destroy
what remained.

After years of silence
the hat box opens

and words thought lost
appear from their annealing,

grow peacock wings,
head north to their source.

*Glass-making terms, such as vitric, frit and cullet, reflect the
Sowerby glass-making heritage, which used the peacock's head
as its mark.*

Sadie Writes a Note

In 1907, an advertising campaign offered free cereal
to every woman who would wink at her grocer.

Wanting to be well-presented,
I thought to save on my housekeeping
and use money meant for cereal
to buy myself some rouge.

Not wishing to offend Mr Diamond,
I visited the grocer two blocks down,
after staring into the bathroom mirror
deciding which eye to use.

I did not know it was his first day
and being unaware of the advertisement in question,
he thought me about to faint,
so carried me to a chair.

I did not buy the rouge. He says
he likes the natural bloom on my cheeks
and we needed all our money
to buy the railcar tickets.

Please water the pot plants on Mondays
and pay the window cleaner.
You will see I have left you
six packs of Battle Creek Toasted Corn.

Finding the Plot

The M6 toll road has been built on two and a half million
copies of old Mills & Boon novels to prevent it from cracking.
Daily Telegraph

Natasha opens her eyes.
Where is Simon with his manly physique
that has weakened her knees
these last two years?

And what page is she on?
She's wearing the ditsy pink dress
which means it's Chapter Two
but there's no phone for her to lose,
so the waiter's strong hands
won't linger on her wrist
as it's returned.

And where is her lipstick?
Without a quick touch up
she'll have no trembling
Cupid's bow to pout.

There should be a Tuscan sunset
to show off her silhouette,
but the air is filled with Caribbean spices,
silver notes from a steel band.

Natasha stops a waiter carrying cocktails
and a riding crop, asks him for white wine,
says nothing when a pint of Guinness
is put down on what she thinks is a bedside table
in the middle of the bar.

Next to the glass is a perfumed envelope
addressed to Mark. She's wondering
if she should open it when Simon waltzes by,
twirling a tall blonde into the penultimate page,
the happy ending that used to be hers.

Natasha's reading the letter
when a petite brunette
with pert nose and gentle smile
pulls up a stool, introduces herself
as Kate, says she was expecting Mike's ex-wife
who blows a fuse, so this is a nice surprise.

The tears for Simon don't well up in Natasha's eyes.
Her chin doesn't tremble.
She offers Kate a sip of the pint,
watches the swell of her throat
as she drinks.

The Second Week of the Soap

I buy six bars before the season starts,
just like my dad used to do.
When I get to the trailer I stack them
in the cupboard with my shirts and boots.

Riding back each night, my hands sweating
on the reins, that's what keeps me going,
knowing I'll lather up that second skin,
slick away the work and dirt
so I'm ready for a beer, whatever
I feel like one-pot cooking.

Out here there's an empty pattern
to the days. I figure I like
those second weeks best.
First one, the bar's a virgin,
too big for my hand.

Seven days of soaping and the hard edges
are gone, it glides smoothly over my shoulders,
brings back memories of other bathtubs,
makes me so mellow that sometimes
I open a second bottle after supper,
drink it slowly as the sun goes down.

In the third week
there's a cussedness about it all.
Darn thing slips through my fingers,
flies into a corner and won't be caught.

By the last night it's thin as a ghost,
buckles under my toes
as I push it down the drain.

Today Old Joe told me
he unwraps a new bar ahead of time,
gets them both nice and wet
then squashes the fresh and the old together.

What use is that? How can you know
when the second week starts?

Hood

I found it at the back of the wardrobe,
never connected the faded red, the pointed hood
with what I'd heard. Not even her size,
stretched thin across the shoulders.

When I mentioned it, the hollow in her neck pulsed,
her teeth left deep indents on her lips.
That old cloak. I should donate it to a jumble
but no-one would want it.

And so it hung between my winter jackets
and her summer dresses. I glimpsed
its shape sometimes while she was dressing,
until the charity bag fell on the mat.

Two pairs of my old trousers, those shoes in mismatched
leather, a couple of finished novels. When I suggested
the cloak her hands clawed at her skirt.
Not now. Not yet. By lunchtime it had gone.

I thought of how we met. Her teenage journey
across borders which brought her to my town.
The months she served me coffee and practised
her English homework when I placed my order.

That first night when I took her home.
The softness of her skin, her saucer eyes,
the way she clung to me when she cried
us both awake with her forest dreams.

Returning late last night, I slipped beneath our duvet
to find the old felt rough across her shoulders,
bitter breath, teeth drawing blood from our kiss
before she slunk from the bed and into the night.

Mattress

She scatters her words across me.
Intensely, celeriac, cyclonic, corpuscular.
Sometimes she brings cheese and biscuits,
sometimes there's the trauma of unmatched
pillows.

His side smells of money, notes press
close to the springs, try to gather dust.
It never lasts.

Wednesday afternoons he's the beachmaster,
makes me creak, bounce his betrayal.

When she sits alone, cross-legged,
all my benthic history seeps out.

She writes late into the night
when he doesn't answer the phone,
rubs her unwashed feet in his hollow.
There's ink on her Garibaldi blouse.

His key hits the door,
his kissmouth puckers towards her.
Afterwards, more words.
Burlesque, sealskin, roquefort.

Twenty Eight Miles from the Russian Tearoom

There is a smell of mould
and mothballs around his neck.
I picture his head hanging
in the wardrobe, me
raising an iced glass to his lips,
washing down macadamia nuts
while I tell him his daughter has stopped
wanting to be a nun
and last week bought a leotard.

When he asks me to sing
I remind him that the date is not even,
so we agree to hum a Latvian folk song instead.

I shall miss these visits but not the form-filling,
each weekly report with its tick against no change.

First Foot

The open fire scalds cold cheeks
scraped raw by old man's stubble.
Numb hands raise last year's sherry,
an eggy snowball, cherry on a sword. Cheers.

The front room's a fug of pipes and fags,
lily of the valley thick and sweet
as the slippered hostess
scuffs in, scuffs out,
keeps plates laden, kettle on the boil.
Men stare at fancy napkins,
down black bun, crunch Twiglets.

One side of Jim Reeves
and coats are back on,
shoulders ready for the blast.
Orra best. Aye, next year.
If we're spared.

Playing Dominoes in Slamannan

Everything the colour of cauliflower.
Sipping pints, vodka and orange,
the taste of posset.

He's thinking of pyjama bottoms,
the walk home,
how some people climb mountains.

This morning's fat storm lingers,
feels like her fingers are growing
beyond the knuckles.

What he needs is a pushy button,
some numbers that match,
but he's chapping.

On the wall a dog pushes a pram.
Her dreams curl up to die,
lipstick still amazing.

Behind the Swing Doors

He's all over the place this morning,
orders flying in, every table full.
Bev and Carolina weave between the faces,
managing expectations, sorry for your wait.

Bacon hisses, he backflips an egg,
turning toast in between, tosses fruit
in the blender for the house special,
Sunshine C, grabs two of the juiciest
strawberries, eats one, pushes
the other between Carolina's red lips.

A smattering of salad garnish
and the breakfast platter's done.
He throws more bacon in the pan,
scratches his nose, what's next?
Time for a quick slash before he fans
smoked salmon on the square white plates.

When Table 10 returns the fruit medley,
complaining to Bev of crumbs,
he drops two new handfuls in a glass bowl,
gets back to the Full Northumbrian.

The woman from head office comes in
with her clipboard and pen.
He gives her the thumbs up
and she ticks the box,
chef wearing gloves.

Uncles

They came in different shapes and smiles.
Some wore suits, the pockets heavy
with keys and coins and sometimes
they'd spin a half-crown, let you keep it.

Their glasses were giant Lego windows
and sometimes they brought aunties
who tried to kiss you, offered
Everton mints from their handbags.

Uncles tried to play football,
holding down their striped ties
with one hand, swerving round
the flower beds, shouting *goal,*

kicking with laced-up leather
that they'd polish with spit
in the living room
when they crossed their legs.

Uncles brought a list of questions
about school and little sisters,
about homework and green vegetables
but never listened to your answers.

And sometimes after Scouts
when it was raining, they'd pull up,
pat the front passenger seat, pull out
a clean white hanky to dry you down.

The Kitchen Storm

He wakes to the sound of rain,
jumps down each step in time to the gusts
against the landing window,
finds his dad in an apron
making the bacon spit up a storm,
cracking shells, thundering
eggs into the blue and white bowl
ready for a beating.

He looks at the table with its three plates,
feels his heartbeat move
to his head, his tongue, his ears,
a drumming so loud he hardly hears the bell,
can't make out the first words she says
when he opens the door to find her dry
on the doorstep, bending to kiss him,
her cheeks still smelling of pillows.

He stares as she picks up the teapot
all wrong, gives him too much milk
in a plain mug, keeps Tigger for herself,
raises it to meet *World's Best Dad*
with its chipped rim, the two of them
kissing so hard they don't notice
the splashes of tea darkening the cloth,
making his toast wet.

One Hundred Ways with Mince

You were, you reminded me,
a second cousin, removed before birth
from Scotland to America.

While the grown-ups chatted
we disappeared with your chemistry set,
the promise of bombs.

Twenty years on, we glossed over
our teenage encounters, the way you mocked me
for not knowing the meaning of *crap* or *gay*.

You mixed me your time-saving blend –
ground coffee, sugar, dried milk –
then told me you knew one hundred recipes for mince.

I was cooking bolognaise for my kids
when I got the call.
Sudden. No pain.

It's made me reckless with my ingredients,
tossing raisins, mint, apple
into the seared meat and onions.

I'm nowhere near one hundred, but last night
I made your special coffee, watched it drip
like tears, turning the glass jug gold.

Casting Off

To him she's still his little firecracker.
Fifty four years her body has cosied him
through the night and though
he does the warming now
he's not complaining.

He feeds her chocolate mousse
while they watch the breakfast news.
Two velvet spoonfuls are all she can manage
most days, so he finishes off the pot
while she's dozing.

All she wants is to finish off her knitting
but the drugs make her dreamy,
the needles so heavy
they send his ruby ring spinning like a planet
round the bone of her finger.

Now he's obsessed with plain and purl,
lingers by her bed, just one more row.
Once she helped him
pick up a lost stitch,
but not today.

The wool is a silken mix, the label says.
It's soft as her pale skin in his hands.
She chose the sassy blue, told him,
a scarf to see you through the winter.
He joins ends in a clumsy knot,
starts on the last ball.

Three Hours after Breaking the News

I am comforted by the weight
of her foot against my leg.
Even though she turned over, clung
to the edge of the bed,
cried herself to sleep,
her foot has crept over,
we are skin to skin.

I can feel the smooth pink of her arch,
the rough thickening of her heel.
Where will it take her?

If I inch my arm across, my hand
will touch her hair. Without looking
I know it will be wild across the sheet,
tangled in the morning.

If she has forgiven me when she wakes,
I will ask her to stretch back, let
her hair fall like stranded seaweed,
use my fingers to tease out the knots,
rub coconut oil into her roots and temples.

How many days will I wake with her here?
Now I've told her, it feels final, though they say
no-one's journey is the same.

Tonight I will celebrate each pain,
each wide awake hour,
for in her sleep she is touching me.

Passing Through

East coast haar presses against the carriage window,
the red letters of arrivals and departures disappear.

Near the steps my grandmother waits with her neighbour.
A day in Dundee, lunch at Draffens.

My mother is waving goodbye. She does not know
this man, filling the doorway of the troop train, will not return.

A five-year-old me in best coat holds my godmother's hand.
When we cross the bridge, steam will engulf us.

By the time we reach the other side
our train will be gone.

Returning

We waited all week for Saturday,
walked across fields with our auntie's ticket
to read and return stories
we still carry with us.

Yesterday we looked for the library
and the village green, the familiar
façade of Washington Electricals,
found a bypass, all our familiar routes
blocked off.

When we reached our house
there were other people
busy in our memories.
We couldn't stay.

But there was still a shop,
with ice cream to eat
and a bus stop to wait at,
even if we didn't know the numbers
or the routes they would take us.

All Around the Day Continues

For this she swapped her well-washed bra
for the starched lace number
that's prickling her shoulders.

For this she deforested her upper lip,
squinted at the mirror to apply mascara,
cut short a client's meeting.

When he offers her olives
she tastes 1975, Germolene.
A sip of wine leaves an aftertaste
of herring, bigger than a baby's head.

She cannot find a reply
to the saga of bespoke dinner plates,
rugby club guttering, copes better
with unseasonal melting of polar ice.

Coffee, the relief of almost leaving
and then he reminds her of Tom Petty,
that April evening and the missed train,
her sister's borrowed shoes.

She looks at his shining head, remembering
the sway of his shoulder length hair,
looks too long into his eyes,
those espresso eyes.

Encounter, 1979

We met in Amsterdam,
his Irish vowels, my Scots lilt,
discussed the cheapest all-day travel,
ate erwten soup in the youth hostel café.
He bought me a banana.

Someone started the passport game,
mugshots shared. He didn't join in.
When I walked from the girls' dorm
for a midnight wee,
he and a man I'd never seen fell silent.

That night a crowd gathered round the television.
A Dutch suburban street.
The British diplomat's car.
In the hostel café,
an empty seat.

Killykeen

I thought *mice*, was ready
to complain to the log cabin owner,
then you saw movement in the 2am sky.
Squeezing sleep-warmed feet into boots
I followed you to the door.

They flew from the trees,
a black veil loosed in the wind,
kept shape as they soared above
our bedroom skylight, round
to the eaves and found their home.

The manager said *pipistrelles*,
the same each August end,
a nursery where parents taught young to fly.
He offered a refund, a move along the lough
for our final week, but we declined.

Three nights and you were snoring through
the rustle of their return.
I read and reread the same page,
watching the clock like old times
until the last stirrings gave way to silence.

Church Conversion

We sleep higher than the choir.
This is where the heat went on winter evenings,
when women dusted snow off hats
and coins slipped through cold fingers
to roll beneath floorboards,
now covered with kitchen laminate.

Our heads are level with the glass angels,
our view of the graveyard
coloured blue, now red.

Sometimes we are wakened
by the smoke of snuffed out candles
at the backs of our throats.
Sometimes, before dawn,
we are convinced
we have been singing.

Each time we walk downstairs
we see the carved poppies.
Our children recite the names,
remember them.

After a shower visitors say
their hair and skin have never felt
so clean and even when
there is no breeze,
my lines of spotless sheets
still billow and blow.

Once, doing dishes, I saw
a dark box reflected in the kitchen window.
Shapes grew round it in the condensation,
moved slowly past the cooker,
disappeared through the fridge freezer
with its closed double doors.

The Cricieth Headsquare

She is waiting for the Number 3 to Pwllheli.
A headsquare patterned with horseshoes
protects her hair from the rain.

Further down the bus queue,
a pink flowered version peeps out
of its owner's pocket.

You are happy to be walking
through a town where headsquares are worn.
You grew up in a world where they were *de rigueur*.

A headsquare was practical, had style,
it was the gift for every occasion.
Shops displayed trays of them all year round.

Umbrellas were too cumbersome, too wet.
They gusted in the lightest wind,
left no hands free for shopping.

Headsquares kept ears cosy,
disguised tired perms,
were favoured by film stars, and the Queen.

Even the Bunty Annual advised
a silk one round a brush
would bring sheen to a young girl's hair.

Headsquares were cloaks for dressing up,
a sling for a broken arm.
They repaired Jack and Jill heads without stitches.

Pulled from your mother's drawer,
their soft warmth smelled of hairspray
with a hint of powder and scent.

You feel chill November in your hair
as you watch the women leave.
Both ears nip, your umbrella spokes have snapped.

Two doors down, a charity shop is raising funds.
It's for a good cause, you reason,
digging through the accessories box.

Wedding Anniversary on the North Sea

You were ill in the Commodore Suite.
The wind outside was a violin.
I took a book and your coat
to the top deck bar.

The wreath sat on a chair
like a sailor's hat
until the singing started and
I followed the crowd outside.

Someone handed me a hymn sheet
in a language I did not know.
Next to me a man wiped his eyes,
a woman cried.

Someone rang a bell,
one note, repeated into the grey,
that carried the wreath
to the white-flecked sea.

I was veiled with spray
by the last amen,
returned to tell of my morning,
while you kissed salt from my hand.

Sobranie

Cocktail colours to match their dresses
or black Russian to match a mood.

These were women whose daughters
I knew at school. They waited
at the gates with impatient car keys,
made meat paste sandwiches
when I came to play.

But Thursday night,
when it was my mother's turn,
they were film stars carrying
wrapped plates like a prize,
draping their scented jackets
over my pegged blazer,
laughing and tossing back their heads
as they entered the living room
which tonight was the lounge,
with the table cleared and polished,
glass coasters, bowls of nuts
and there, in the centre, the Sobranies,
to be offered round with martinis,
red or white.

One cigarette each,
once a week,
on Thursday night.

I Loved the Old Festival Hall Toilets

Because they weren't well sign-posted
so there was never a queue.

Because of their honeyed wood walls
scented with Max Factor compacts.

Because I warmed to the pitted taps
that scalded my winter hands

and learned how to make the toilet chain
begin a reluctant flush.

Because of the mirrors,
jewelled by generations of lacquered perms,

their dull fluorescence
never reflecting wrinkles.

Because of my mother's voice
when I told her where I was

and found her stiletto imprints
in the dark linoleum.

Mrs Thorpe's Arithmetic

A new term and we are adding beetroot and fig.
If a man bought the last of the spring onions.
We calculate the length of runner beans,
divide up soup ingredients
while her muddy hands mark papers.

Christmas gifts of pomegranates challenge us
to crack leather skin, count jewel seeds.
In February we make get well cards,
she sends blood oranges and a sum.
If a man had three artichokes, took away one.
We deliver summer peaches
to her hospital bed, tally up our tomatoes.

Today her rhythm of fruit and veg
multiplies with my children. Here are peas
falling from a pod, next month we pick sweetcorn.
Everything has its season.

In *Life Story*

the parts of wise old woman
and annoying voice on the phone
are played by her mother,
long-suffering husband is represented
by sighs and silence, the occasional cough.

Embarrassed, do-we-*have*-to-be-in-this children
were played by little people whose bedroom doors
are now firmly shut.

The man she sometimes thought about
was the sexy voice in the dream sequence,
cut short when his balding head
appeared in the supermarket queue.

The part of best friend is shared, depending
on time of the month and latest texts,
although each believes she has the leading role.

Understanding doctor remains vacant
and casting continues for the perfect boss.

Young self was played following two glasses of wine,
the optimist after four,
older but no wiser the next morning
accompanied by two paracetamol and a black coffee.
The cigarette in earlier drafts has been extinguished.

Music is that song on the radio
she can't stop humming
and the script written by someone who hoped
for more laughs and a bigger pay cheque.

Life Story, recorded on location,
is an On-Going Production.

Inviolata

Near the end
she said she could feel
her bones go,
pictured
iridescent shells
in pieces,
the fragmented skeleton
of a wren.

This, she said,
was necessary,
so the morning breeze
could carry her
through the open window,
over trees and traffic,
to where bodies don't matter
anymore.